DULCE

DULCE

Anglo Family Life
on the
Jicarilla Apache Reservation

Patricia Williams Lein

SANTA FE
NewMexico

First Edition

Printed in the United States of America

10 9 8 7 6 5 4 3 2 1

Library of Congress Cataloging in Publication Data:

Williams Lein, Patricia, 1935-

    Dulce: Anglo family life on the Jicarilla Apache Reservation / Patricia Williams Lein.

    p.   cm.

    ISBN 0-86534-207-5 : $10.95

    1. Jicarilla Indians. 2. Williams Lein, Patricia, 1935- 3. Jicarilla Indian Reservation
(N.M.) 4. Indian agents—New Mexico. 5. New Mexico—Biography.   I. Title
E99.J5W45   1993
978.9'52—dc20   93-23522
                                                          CIP

Published by   SUNSTONE PRESS
                  Post Office Box 2321
                  Santa Fe, NM 87504-2321 / USA
                  (505) 988-4418 *orders only* (800) 243-5644
                  FAX (505) 988-1025

ACKNOWLEDGMENTS

I want to thank my entire family, for their support, love, encouragement, and efforts on my behalf while I worked endlessly on this book—Sharon, Ruth, and Chris Williams, who helped me many hours with stories and photos, Janice Lein and Ken Butler who spent many hours on the computer, and the Webber and Associates, Inc., and Roy, for his patience when I needed it most. I also want to thank Agapita Abeyta, for her support, and the Jicarilla Apaches for their history. I want to mention my children who always believed in my success, Stephen, Mark, David and Pamela, and of course my highest praise goes to my creator, Almighty God, who is in charge.

Patricia Williams Lein

INTRODUCTION

My primary reason for writing this book, was a burning desire to bring to this wonderful country, a lively up-beat story, based on true life experiences of my family on the Jicarilla Apache Indian Reservation, in Dulce, New Mexico, during the period of 1938 to 1942.

My father, Al Williams, worked for an agency of the Bureau of Indian Affairs, as a postmaster, accountant and advisor to the Jicarillas. His magnetism and charisma gained him the honorary title of Chief Red Eagle from the members of the Apache council.

My early exposure to the Apaches provided me with the power to overcome many obstacles and trials in my own life. Their quiet determination, subtle humor and strength, had a lasting influence on my entire family.

Indian nations all throughout the United States should receive the praise, respect and support they deserve, if for no other reason, than they were the very first Americans. It is my desire also to preserve and document our history during that era.

I have changed some names in the stories to protect surviving relatives as well as to avoid disturbing the resting spirits of my Apache friends.

Patricia Williams Lein

Chapter
1

It was 1940 and I was five years old. I walked along the dirt road, watching carefully where I stepped, because many horses and wagons had traveled through this little town of Dulce, New Mexico. Dad used to say, "Whoops, better watch out for the horse doopers!"

Deep ruts were etched in the dirt road, dug by heavy wagons loaded with supplies to feed the Jicarilla Apache Indians, who lived nearby on the reservation. My father, Al Williams, worked for an agency of the Bureau of Indian Affairs and his job was to act in several capacities such as postmaster, accountant, advisor and friend to the Jicarillas. Of course, to me he was the most important man in the world!

The Apaches loved him and held him in very high esteem. He truly acted in their behalf and grew to be great friends with many of the Indians on the reservation. He understood and respected their culture and spent long hours trying to untangle bureaucratic red tape in their favor.

My father was charming and extremely handsome. He had black wavy hair and recognizable Indian features due to his being a quarter Cherokee. He was a very fine family man. We were very important to him, and remained so, throughout his entire life. His good looks were often a worry to Mother. She was sometimes jealous of the attention he received from other females, but she reasoned that, "Others could look and appreciate, but not touch."

Dad found this form of jealousy much to his liking. He was a charmer sure enough. But I knew if any other woman tried to encroach on Mother's territory, he would quickly put a "quietus" on it. (That was the special word he used for stopping anything he did not wish to continue.)

I was on my way to the trading post to see if my little brother was there. My older sister, Sherry, stayed at home helping my mother. Fellow ran away from home on a regular basis looking for adventure. We called him Fellow, because I looked at him when he was born and commented, "Isn't he a cute little fellow." It stuck, and he had to grow up with that nickname.

Fellow was always turning over every stone and log looking for anything that caught his interest. Once he found an entire family of skunks, and placed one on his head. He walked around for hours with that tiny creature on his head and when Mother found him, she was horrified. "How will I ever get this smell out of your hair!" She had to burn his clothes, and I didn't think she was ever going to let him back in the house again.

It was a beautiful day in the mountains. The spring air was crisp and cool. A slight breeze felt pleasant against my face and as I looked up, the clouds of a recent rain were exposing a brilliant cerulean blue sky and a warm sun ready to break through. The rain shower left little puddles, like mirrors, reflecting their surroundings. The wet sod had a pungent smell which made me wonder how it would taste. Spring was wonderful in the Northern New Mexico mountains. Its beauty is hard to describe to anyone who has never experienced it.

I heard a meadowlark sing an engaging song in a nearby field. A shiver of excitement passed through me. What a great place to live! Off in the distance, the view of the Rocky mountains was breath taking. Snow still capped the highest peaks bringing back memories of rapturous days spent sledding down steep banks in the cold snow, and later drinking hot chocolate around a bonfire that comforted our nearly frozen hands and feet.

As I approached an old bridge that spanned the arroyo, (a big ditch or "gully"), I suddenly felt an uncomfortable fear. I had never really told anyone how much I hated to cross that creaky old thing, especially now that the Spring run off from the mountains was causing the arroyo to swell with rapidly rising water. It was only wide enough for one wagon to travel across at a time, and any poor soul caught walking across it when a wagon was using it, had to press up against the wooden rails that seemed to lean dangerously and maliciously toward the raging water below.

It was always my bad luck to be in the middle of the rotten span when that very thing happened. It was only about fifteen feet wide, with badly worn bottom boards that were full of splinters and holes. How could it possibly withstand the abuse of heavy wagons and horses over the years?

As I started across, I saw a wagon nearing. Damn, just my luck! It was drawn by two horses seemingly pulling against each other for leadership. I felt my stomach churning and my heart thumping, all the while trying to talk myself out of sheer panic. I felt my body becoming one with those rotten side rails. The driver was totally unaware of my fear and he snapped the reins against the rump of his team.

Dad had advised us to always be polite when passing our Indian friends. He had even taught us a greeting which I feebly attempted to use. I stammered out "Tonjo jo ney," which could barely be heard about the thundering feet of the racing horses. I could almost reach out and touch their flanks as they raced across the old bridge. But the wagon loaded with supplies and several Indian children passed by without any harm to me. I noticed, as it disappeared down the road that the Indian children seemed to have laughing eyes. Were they making fun of me, or just enjoying my greeting? I never knew, but they lifted their hands to wave so I felt better about the whole experience.

My speeding heart returned to normal and the trading post was now in sight. Quickly walking across the road and up the old board steps, I noticed, just beyond the end of the long wooden front porch, an Indian man was sprawled in the dirt walkway with his feet and legs sticking out into the road. I recognized him as the town drunk and the reservation "bad man." He was by reputation the meanest man around and always drinking, hence his name—Fire Man. People, wagons, cars and animals passed by without even a glance in his direction. "Oh no! Maybe he is dead!" I thought. I hurried into the store without looking back.

I was greeted by many eyes. Well, Mother was right. There sat Fellow perched up on the counter, stuffing his mouth with candy given in return for repeating swear words that sounded vaguely like gutter words, but not so much as to be positive. The Indian men were laughing uproariously over every little syllable as though they really understood what he was saying. Ish Koten's favorite phrase was, "shus pe toh," which he explained was translated as "little bear turd," but we were never sure. Ish Koten was the town sheriff and sheriff of all the Apaches as well.

I greeted my father as he came from his office to see what all the ruckus was about. Putting his arm around me, he hugged me and thanked me for coming after Fellow. "He will never learn correct English around here." This statement, said goodnatured, brought more laughter.

Dad lifted Fellow down from the counter and told me to take him home. He gave him a stern scolding but we both knew it probably wouldn't do much good. Fellow was definitely born for adventure.

Before we could leave, I was handed a bottle of orange soda by Ish Koten, who was one of my favorite friends. His dedication to his people, fairness, bravery and concern for the welfare of others, won loyalty and friendship from most of the towns people along with that of the Jicarilla Apaches.

He dressed more like the towns people than he did the Indians. He always wore a huge velour hat and a faded cowboy shirt with pearl buttons, ill-fitting jeans, held up by a wide leather belt and fascinating silver and turquoise buckle, and of course the all-important black boots. He was full-blood Apache, dark skinned and tall. His eyes were full of merriment, and teasing us seemed to his dedicated goal. Sometimes he would pull ribbon candy out of his shirt pocket, and other times he would jump on the back bumper of our car, making the car bounce up and down furiously like a bucking horse. We loved it!

He kept the peace as well as any man could. No one really ever knew much about his private life. He would not reveal anything about his past, but one thing was for certain, he knew his job well.

My father used to tell this story about Ish Koten's bravery. Once Ish Koten and his friend Joseph Bear were riding horseback through the mountains searching for a marauding cougar that had been raiding sheep herds and prowling dangerously close to the tepees on the reservation. As they passed under a tall pine tree, the lurking cougar leaped on to the horse, knocking Joseph to the ground.

Ish Koten's horse was spooked too, and it reared and threw him to the ground, leaving him unable to reach his rifle. The big cat was already hell-bent on attacking Joseph, who was on his back, kicking with both legs as hard as he could. Ish Koten grabbed a nearby fallen tree limb and beat the angry mountain cat around the head and shoulders until it decided to make an escape. According to Dad's story, that cat is still running.

But back to the present. I said good-bye to our friend and my father and took fellow by the hand and started for home. I had to drag him at first because he was reluctant to come under his own steam. We both waved again as we neared the bridge. Ish Koten called out "Tish a Heh ten ya." I didn't know what that meant in Apache, but I assumed it was friendly.

Dad was watching from the doorway of the trading post, so we felt more secure about crossing the bridge. No one noticed a horse drawn wagon, with a large hayrake attached to the back, standing unattended near the side of the store. Something must have alarmed the horses that moment and they bolted straight for the bridge, dragging the dangerous hayrake from side to side like a giant sickle. We were in a perilous position.

My father ran as fast as he could and managed to place himself in front of the speeding horses and started to wave his arms and yell frantically. This turned the run-a-way horses back toward the center of the road and they ran to the end of the street before being stopped by the owner. We were safe.

As our badly shaken father helped us across the bridge, he could not help but notice that the arroyo had risen significantly since morning.

Chapter
2

Every spring we were threatened by flooding because an arroyo ran directly behind our house. To make matters worse, the land around our house was lower than the rest of Dulce, making high water in the yard a regular thing. So far, in the three years we had lived in Dulce, we had escaped flood water in the house but I had seen it at the very top of the banks and licking at the old boards of the bridge.

I looked up at the sky where the clouds were building up again. I had heard Dad talking to Mother this morning, "Sure does look like we are in for trouble with the arroyo this year. Better pack a trunk Ruth, in case of an emergency. We might have to move to higher ground this spring."

I tried not to feel afraid about the impending run off, but deep in my heart I knew the signs of a serious problem brewing. When I got home with the little varmint in tow, Mother thanked me and seemed relieved that someone had even a small measure of control over Fellow's actions. She asked me how the arroyo looked and I noticed a ring of worry in her voice.

It was beginning to get dark now, as night came early in the mountains during the winter and early spring months. Mother started to pace the floor. My father wasn't home yet!

It had started to rain again—this time drumming down hard enough to build up on the road that passed in front of the house. We did not have a telephone. In fact, very few people in Dulce had phones. They could be any place in five minutes by walking, so there was really no great need. But at times like this, it would have been very helpful to be able to pick up a phone and say "Where the devil are you Al? I'm scared to death and I want you home!"

Mother found a flashlight and went to the back door, peering out to see if she could determine how bad the situation was. She decided to venture out toward the arroyo just a little, to get a glimpse. The arroyo was about one hundred yards from the back of the house and was fenced off by three strands of barbed wire. (The barbed wire did not stop us, however, when we decided to break the house rules and sneak over or through it to snake hunt or throw stones at the water.) We were never allowed to play near it, even in the summer when it was bone dry.

Mother walked away from the house and we could not see her except for the erratic darting of the light from the flashlight she carried. Sherry pulled us back from the door just as a flash of lightening made everything bright as day. We could see Mother running back toward the house. Dashing through the door, not even taking time to shake the rain from her rain coat, she began to issue firm orders.

"Sherry, grab that stack of blankets and put them up on the dining table. Patsy, get Fellow into his rain coat and don't let him out of your sight. I think we're going to have to make a run for it. I'm going to try to reach the barn to get the car, but I'm not sure we can get through. Oh mercy, where is Al?"

Panic struck me. I was sure we were going to be swept away by the raging arroyo. There was no time to sob now, so I swallowed my tears. Mother was running around quickly trying to secure as much as she could, and giving orders like a top sergeant.

Fellow stuck close to me now. I placed my arm around his shoulder and drew him closer, as much for my own comfort as his. We all heard the sound of a big truck engine at the same time. God had answered our prayers again.

Men's voices were shouting and Dad came bursting through the door. He had been watching the arroyo all day and had already made plans to move us to higher ground regardless.

By the time they backed the truck into the drive, muddy swirling water was covering the boardwalk from the front part of the house and lapping at the porch itself. My father was anxious to get us over the road and back across the bridge before all the landmarks were gone. If he drove off the road we would slide down embankments to the pasture land and to certain drowning, or even go off into the swift arroyo.

The truck was huge. It had large wheels and when the water was up to the top of the hubcaps, we knew time was everything now. The men quickly carried us out, along with the trunk, and placed us safely in the back of the truck bed. Mother climbed up beside us and the three men scrambled into the cab. The truck started right up and Dad found his way carefully back down the road which was now covered completely with water, swirling limbs and trash. He made his way by watching for fence posts, large rocks and the bridge rails.

Everywhere we looked we could only see tops of things that we once took for granted. We heard the water sloshing up against the bottom of the truck bed but we were not afraid anymore. The truck carried us to safety and we spent the night with friends.

Eventually I became resentful of the fact that other people in Dulce had warmer safer homes, and closer to school than ours. But Dad would always explain it away by saying, "Do you think they have as much fun, or as much love as we have here?" We were warm enough, but having to heat with a coal burning potbellied stove, while some of my friends bragged about furnaces, made me jealous.

Sometimes during the winter, we were allowed to move into a government house when a family had vacated it to go to Albuquerque or Santa Fe, but no more than a few months.

Dad was not actually a government employee because he worked for an agency that worked for the government. It was all confusing to me.

The superintendent of the bureau kept a stern and watchful eye on the rules and regulations and we were denied many things because of the technicality of Dad's working for the store, rather than directly for the bureau. But it did not effect our comfort. My father saw to that.

Chapter
3

Summer came, and with it Mother's annual desire to raise chickens. This drove Dad wild. He hated chickens, both seeing them and eating them. He was raised on a farm in Oklahoma and his disgust for barnyard chickens knew no bounds. But he gave in and brought home one hundred baby chicks for her to raise. He even brought two lambs for us to have as pets and we added those to the household dog, Corky.

The brooder was attached to the north end of the barn. We were told to keep out of that area because the new chicks had to be kept in a warm environment for a few weeks. But temptation overcame good judgement and we crawled into the brooder by way of the trap door to play with the chicks.

They were entertaining and we watched them wiggle away from our grasp, run erratically all over the brooder floor, jumping in the watering trough, and scampering through the feed tray. I guess we did squeeze some of them a little to tightly but no harm came from that. It was our leaving the trap door open, that did most of them in. The cool night mountain air was deadly to the poor little critters, and most of them died.

To say that we were in deep trouble with Dad is an understatement. He was very angry and determined to spank all three of us. We deserved it, but Mother came to our rescue and forbid him to spank us. She reasoned that "what was done, could not be undone." She said she was sure we had learned our lesson. We heard this statement many times after that.

But Dad, intent on vindicating the dead chickens and delivering those swats to someone, pulled Mother down across his lap and pretended to give them to her. We found this funny (probably a nervous reaction). Not Mother! She immediately packed a suit case for the four of us. My father, seeing that he was in big trouble, begged and pleaded for forgiveness. He apologized over and over but it fell on deaf ears.

We were rushed into the Lincoln and Mother drove to Chama, a small town north of Dulce, where we spent that night in the local hotel. She was very cross with us and intent on teaching Al Williams a lesson.

Later the following day, she decided to return to Dulce. When we got home, we found a very sad husband and father sitting in a chair with tears rolling down his face. I never saw him cry again, and peace once again reigned in the Williams' household.

My love and respect for my father was boundless. He was not a violent man, and rarely felt inclined to spank any of us. He was good at reasoning and it usually only took a stern look to stop us in our tracks. I believe this air of respect and dignity was responsible for much of his success with the Jicarillas.

Chapter
4

My Parents were never separated again except for circumstances beyond their control, such as the time Dad was lost in the freezing mountains for two days.

We had good friends named Beth and Fred Lyons who lived on a beautiful ranch nestled high in the mountains near Dulce. They had invited the entire family up for the weekend and Dad and Fred were going deer hunting.

The prospect of spending a weekend on this particular ranch was pure elation to me. I loved it there and could hardly wait until time to start the trip. It was early November and we had not had a very heavy snow yet, just flakes and flurries. It was bitter cold at night though, so we were warmly dressed and prepared in case a big snow came that weekend. Snow was not unusual in that area and we were always well equipped.

We made our way to the ranch on a well traveled old road that seemed to wind forever through the mountains. With one curve after another, through deep ruts, we could see a panoramic view that was breathtaking. Sometimes there were sheer drops to the canyon below and at other times, views of the highest snow capped peaks. The road was narrow and steep and only wide enough for one car to pass. I wondered if this was one of the original roads that my grandfather, Daniel Beal, built using basic tools, mules and a big scoop-like device called a fresno. My grandmother traveled with him in a covered wagon to help with the cooking and keep him company. It was a rugged life but she loved it.

Snow had fallen during the night, but patches of dirt road could still be seen here and there. The snow had settled on the branches of the hundreds of tall pines and fir trees. It looked like a wonderland. There was a special excitement about the stillness of the mountains and knowing at that moment, we were enjoying it totally alone.

The Lincoln, my father's pride and joy, hummed along hugging the old ruts. Dad said it was safer on the road than any other car. That was meant to make us feel more secure and it did. Especially now, when curve after curve took us higher up the mountain.

The majestic, age old pines gave the appearance of tall sentinels, guarding the gates to heaven. The artistic combination of glittering white snow against the dark evergreen of the needles, could not be captured except by the imagination.

Finally, we reached the top and the road leveled out to meadow and smaller trees. We were able to see the ranch house in the distance. It was well guarded by trees. Barbed wire fences were on both sides of the road, held up by old twisted fence posts. A hawk sat perched on the top of one of the posts, watching every move as we passed by.

Hereford cattle stood passively in the pasture. During the winter, they were fed hay that was harvested and stored in large barns. Ranchers could not always count on natural vegetation to feed them when the ground was covered with heavy layers of snow and ice. They could withstand the low temperatures but not starvation.

An imposing windmill was standing silent in the quiet atmosphere. There was a circular, slightly rusted water tank where the cattle congregated to drink and the ground around the tank was well trampled from the many heavy hooves.

Dad stopped the car and got out to open the large wooden gate that kept the cattle in and strangers out. He was met by the happy bark of Wolf, the Lyons family dog. This name was from his wolf-like appearance. His fur was long and fluffy grey, which was a contrast to his white pointed face and magnificent piercing amber eyes.

Wolf was glad to see my father because they had become lasting friends over the years when Fred would bring him into town in the back of his pickup truck to get the mail and supplies for the ranch. Dad always gave Wolf a pat on the head and scratched him affectionately behind his ears.

Dad called for Mother to drive the Lincoln through and he closed the gate behind the car. As we approached the ranch house, with Wolf racing ahead of us, we saw Beth waiting on the porch.

It was a long porch, extending the entire length of the front of the house. There were various rockers and chairs and a table at one end that was used for evening deserts and late dinners.

Beth waved and called for us to get out and come in. "It's so good to see you." She was very pretty, half Apache and half Anglo. Fred was not Indian, and they made a great couple.

Beth ushered us into the main living room which was spacious and inviting with huge rafters. A wagon wheel had been made into a light fixture which hung from the ceiling and there were Indian rugs on the old, but carefully tended wooden floor. Beth and Fred had gathered the stones and rocks and built the immense fireplace themselves.

The hearth was raised about a foot and served as a shelf for various objects. There was a loaded rifle over the mantle. The fireplace being all stone, brought the history and age of the mountains in the living room. It was already hard at work giving off a cheerful and inviting glow.

Mounted over the mantle was a deer's head. I avoided looking directly at its soft eyes for I was sure it was still alive. In spite of the deer's head, I was convinced that this had to be the most inviting room I had ever been in.

I could visualize many wonderful nights with the family gathered around the roaring fire listening to Fred talk about his adventures in this rugged country.

Off to the left was the kitchen, a huge room. It was of great interest to me now because I was beginning to feel very hungry. I could smell the delicious aroma of beef cooking and something spicy—apple pie?

Beth's daughter, Sara, lead us to the right and up some stairs to a landing which led to the sleeping area. She chattered all the while about how happy she was to have some friends her age to play with. She was young and I'm sure life got very lonely for her at times in such isolation.

She explained that her father had gone to retrieve some horses from the back pasture for tomorrow's hunting trip. He would be back soon. We were lead to Sara's room first where a large double bed greeted us. It was high off the floor and had large posters towering almost to the ceiling. I could imagine how much fun that was going to be—three girls in a bed talking all night and telling ghost stories. If you have never slept three in a bed and talked until the wee hours of the morning, you have missed one of life's greatest and most enriching experiences.

Beth showed Mother and Dad to their sleeping quarters which was a few doors away from ours. Thank goodness, because my father was very fussy if he was awakened during the night with giggles and noise. I have seen his very stern and gruff expression many nights when we had "sleepover" friends and got carried away with our stories. He would appear in our door and we knew he meant business.

Beth had a flare for southwestern decor, and it was just as inviting in the bedrooms as it was in the main living area of the house. The center of attention in each room was the large beds with the big posters. They were massive and strong. Everything smelled of clean blankets and oiled wood, and of course, the smell of apple pie in every square inch of the house.

In the corner of each bedroom was a wash stand holding a pitcher and wash basin. Sara explained that sometimes in the winter, during zero weather, they were forced to melt snow for washing and drinking until their water pipes could be thawed.

On the floor was an Indian rug about nine feet square. The designs were so intriguing that I never got tired of seeing Indian artistry. In addition to weaving rugs, they could take precious metal out of the ground and pound and shape it into beautiful silver objects. They could take stone like turquoise, onyx and coral and make exquisite bracelets, rings and belt buckles. And they could take clay from the earth and shape it into functional and attractive pots and bowls and drinking vessels.

Indians raised sheep, carded the wool, and then made it into the beautiful rugs, as well as blankets and clothing. I believe them to be one of the most artistic races on earth. They are also, in my opinion, the most spiritually in tune to God's great creation and focus for man. Frequently, designs on blankets, rugs and clothing, depicted some religious story and man's relationship with earth, sky and the "Great Father."

Dulce had a mission that many Indians visited often and they would find many new ways to express their spiritual needs and thoughts. Many, upon converting to Christianity, would give their children new Christian names, like Josef, Lucas, Peter, Mary and Sarah. They were wonderfully trusting, but they never turned their backs on their heritage or culture.

Many Indians were sent to be educated in schools far away from the reservation even though there was an Indian school in Dulce, as well as a hospital just for them. They would become lawyers, teachers, doctors, nurses and musicans and would always return sooner or later, to their homes on the reservation bringing their new skills home to the reservation to share with their people.

After Sara finished getting us settled, she invited us to explore the barn, corral and all the exciting places around their ranch. Dinner would not be ready for another hour and I hated to hear that. My stomach was calling out to that delicious smell coming from the kitchen. But the excitement of exploring new grounds was stronger at that moment so we raced outside to begin our new adventure.

We walked through the cattle pen to the barn and I kept my eye on one old bull in particular. He seemed a bit too interested in me. Sara told us not to be afraid because she walked through here all the time—easy for her to say!

When we reached the barn, the smell of fresh hay and old wood greeted us. We could hear birds fluttering around in the old rafters and the cracks in the siding of the barn let in enough light to make everything seem a little eerie.

We looked into every stall. I sat on Fred's prize horse and had fun swinging on a long rope with a big knot tied in the end to sit on. The rope was hung from the second floor rafters and it would swing out over a huge pile of fresh straw. You could then drop off the rope into the straw and never get hurt. You could hear the rope creaking and pulling against the old wood and wonder how long it had been there. We scrambled up a rickety ladder to the hay loft where we could peer out a small door used for dropping hay bales to waiting wagons below. From that vantage point, we could see almost all around the ranch. It was a view I will never forget.

Finally we heard the unmistakable sound of the dinner bell. We raced for the house, washed our hands and took our place at the long table in the dining room. The ranch cook brought out our meal, and sure enough, my nose had been right on target, roast beef and whipped potatoes in the largest bowl I had ever seen. There was gravy, rich and brown, and hot biscuits served with honey from their own hives. Bits of honeycomb could still be seen floating in the amber colored sweet nectar. The meal was topped off with warm apple pie.

After dinner we sat around the fireplace while Fred and my father exchanged stories about their many experiences at the trading post. All too soon it was time to call it a day and retire. I didn't complain much because I had grown drowsy while listening to the stories and watching the flickering flames in the massive fireplace.

Early the next morning, we saw the men ride out—heavy coats, rifles and hunting gear strapped to the horses' saddles and flanks. They expected to return before night fall but had to plan for cold weather and possible heavy snow. Dad rode the big red quarter horse and Fred was on his prize horse, a handsome bay. "Al has the best tracking horse in this part of the country, Ruth, so don't worry about him. Big Red will take care of him." With a smile and a wave they rode out.

We had the remainder of the day to finish exploring every inch of the ranch. By night fall we were exhausted and hardly noticed that the men were not back yet. Big flakes of snow were falling now. It had just "spritzed" the ground during the day with light snow but now it was serious. It was beginning to drift against the barn and house and the ground was well covered.

Mother expressed a little concern but Beth said that horses were accustomed to snow and did well maneuvering through it. We had heard several rifle shots during the day from the far distance. It was impossible to know where the sound was coming from because sound echoed in the mountains surrounding the ranch. We just assumed that someone had a successful hunt.

As evening approached and night closed in on the ranch, Mother became more and more nervous. She rationalized that the men were warmly dressed, well armed and had food to eat. Beth comforted her by saying "Fred knows these mountains like the back of his hand, Ruth. You will see. They will be riding up any minute. They probably bagged a deer and stopped to dress it out." But she was also beginning to worry.

From the window she saw a rider approaching through the heavy snow—alone. It was Fred. She ran to the door and stepped out onto the long porch, now lightly covered with snow that had blown in under the protective overhang. She didn't seem to notice the cold beneath her feet and around her ankles. "Where is Al?" she asked him. "Let's get in the house Beth, I'm darn near frozen. I'm afraid I have some bad news."

Fred took the bay horse to the barn and trudged quickly through the snow back to the house. Mother's heart was pounding with fear. Fred went straight to her and put his arm around her shoulder to calm her down.

"Ruth, try not to worry now. I'm sure Al is fine. We got separated early on in the hunt and I have spent all day looking for him. I'm afraid he is lost out there. I'm going to drive into Dulce and arrange a search party for early morning. We can't do anything in the dark except get lost ourselves. Al will be fine. He has Big Red and he has matches and his rifle. Red is a smart horse. He can probably find his way back. We'll find Al tomorrow morning, cold, hungry and cussing his head off."

Mother tried not to cry. She knew my father could take care of himself in most cases and that he had been in many tight situations before, but this time he was exposed to sub-zero weather and wild animals.

She went to bed, but sleep did not come. Everyone was up before daybreak watching the road for some encouraging sign of a horse and rider. I'm sure Fred did not sleep at all but kept vigil by the window.

More snow had fallen during the night and it deepened our concern for Dad's safety. I could not help but let a tear escape, but I quickly wiped it away.

Fred drove into Dulce and within a few minutes, had a search party formed. It consisted of many of my fathers friends and part of the Indian council that were familiar with the area.

Someone called Santa Fe and the Rangers sent out a search plane to aid the ground searchers. Fred came back to the ranch after the organization of the search party to get his horse. He could lead the team to the last place that my father was seen.

After lunch Mother could stand it no longer and she insisted that we all go back to Dulce. She would feel better in her own home. Beth tried to talk her out of going but Mother had made up her mind.

She bundled all of us up and packed the Lincoln and started down the snow packed road for home. We inched our way down the mountain. The road was very slippery and there were sheer drops at every curve to the canyon below. The Lincoln had chains and was heavy, which helped.

As we rounded a curve the car started to slide—just a little at first—and then suddenly spun around with its front bumper headed toward the edge looking over the sheer steep drop below, and the back bumper was practically against the cliff or bank as we called it.

I have never been that scared before. Now what do we do? My mother was a very self confident and spunky person, she always seemed to be able to handle whatever life served her. Intimidation was not something she recognized. In fact, when she was a child, she rode a horse five miles to school every day, killed rattlesnakes, drove a car by the time she was twelve, and cared for herself and two older brothers while her mother traveled by covered wagon to help Grandad Beal on roundups and building roads. And she knew just what to do now. She turned off the motor and opened her door and told us to get out and climb up on the bank out of the way of the tires and the car. She explained that she was going to try to turn the car back around and she did not want us in the car in the event the car went over the embankment.

She got back in the car, started the engine and literally, inch by inch went forward than back, turning the wheel slightly until she finally had the car turned around back in the direction of the ranch. She then backed down the slippery road to a place where the terrain leveled out.

She got out of the car and waved for us to come down. We did, slipping, sliding, and laughing all the way.

When we got home we spent the remainder of the day waiting to receive news of Dad. Occasionally someone would come by with an update but we were beginning to hear pessimism in their voices. We prepared for bed and all night I could hear Mother pacing back and forth. By morning she was pale and exhausted. "I feel so helpless," she said. She tried to remain calm for us, but we knew she had just about given up.

My father had been missing now for two days in the freezing mountains. I said a little prayer. "God, please let my father come home soon. I love him and we need him." Mother went through the motions of looking after the house.

Many people came by with encouraging words and offers of food and company for a while. We were grateful for all the people still out in the cold searching for him. Then all of a sudden, without warning, my father appeared in the doorway. I don't have to describe the joy we felt. He was cold, hungry and cussing his head off, just like Fred said he would. After our tearful reunion, he settled down and told his story.

Big Red had literally saved his life. When he became aware that he was hopelessly lost he built a fire to keep him warm through the freezing first night and to keep the animals away. When morning came he attempted to find his way out but only succeeded in getting more confused and finally, totally disoriented.

The temperature had dropped to below zero and he was afraid Big Red could not survive. He knew he could not make it out of those mountains without that horse. He heard the distinct howl of distant wolves so he built the fire up to a roaring blaze and soon drifted off into a troubled sleep, waking off and on throughout the night. He dreamed of hot coffee and his family and the possibility of being eaten alive by wild animals.

When daylight came, he decided that the best thing to do was to just give Big Red his lead and maybe he could find the way out of the canyon. That was a smart move because Big Red did just that. He picked his way carefully along the trail never losing his footing and eventually came upon a clearing and the road where the rescue team found them.

His Indian friends were very happy that they had helped in his rescue. They spent days afterward gathered around the old pot bellied stove in the general store, telling and exchanging jokes and stories of their friend's adventure. Of course the stories grew to magnificent proportions.

Chapter
5

The Indians were very good friends. We received many gifts from them such as beautiful baskets and brightly decorated pots, belts, necklaces, rugs, and food. They would also bring wild game from time to time but I could never be tempted to try elk steaks or bear stew. But my father never seemed to grow tired of these things.

He was held in high esteem by the Jicarillas and at one point they bestowed the honorary title of "Chief Red Eagle" on him. Jim Baltazar, the chief of all the Jicarillas, even offered him another wife. Mother only weighed about one hundred and ten pounds and he could not understand how she could work hard. He said, "Al, you need a fine strong young woman." Mother very quickly squelched that offer. Dad explained that in our culture more than one wife was forbidden, so he accepted the offer of a live-in maid and nanny. My father thanked Jim for his generous gift and from that time on we had a helper around the house. Mother was really not very strong so this was a great help to her.

We had several girls that stayed for a while and then grew tired of our ways and left. Then came Euna. She was mean and abusive. She would slap, pinch, and strike matches in our faces with threats of burning our noses off if we did not obey. She threatened to harm us if we told Mother or my father about any of the abuse. But one day, I could no longer stand it and I told. My parents were both appalled and angry. Euna was immediately discharged and told to never come around our house again. She deserved more of a reprimand than that but in those days the issue of child abuse was just not addressed as it is today.

Unfortunately we were struck by the power of matches and decided to try them out ourselves. Fellow and I took some out to the barn and stacked up little piles of straw and hay. We would strike a match, drop it on the little piles and watch with amazement how it would flare up instantly in the dry straw. It was fascinating, but all of a sudden it roared out of control and could not be stamped out. I grabbed Fellow by the hand and we ran from the barn as quickly as we could and ran right into Mother! She was about as mad as I have ever seen her. She had missed us and decided to come looking for us. Good thing! She grabbed the water hose and quickly put out the raging fire before it could destroy the road equipment or the barn.

The tanks of the expensive road equipment were always full of gasoline and it would have been a disaster if the fire had reached them.

Our punishment was appropriate for this mis-adventure. We were confined to our rooms for days. All we could do was look out the window at the beautiful sunny days and blue sky. We watched our pets roam and play without us and I cannot ever remember being so miserable. I would lay on my bed during the afternoon and listen to the call of the meadowlark in the pasture across the road. I would feel the soft summer breeze blowing gently across my face and long to be outside. We learned our lesson from the match caper.

Chapter
6

After Euna was fired, we employed another Indian girl named Tonita. She was also Apache. We loved her because she was kind and patient with us and talented and playful as well. Tonita would spend hours braiding my hair, telling us stories, cooking our favorite meals and teaching us songs. Fellow had stars in his eyes over her and she became a much loved member of our family.

Tonita had a niece named Delfina who was exactly Sherry's age and she became one of Sherry's good friends. Delfina did not have all the special food, toys and comforts that we had so we gladly shared with her and she was almost like a sister.

Delfina always walked us to school. There was an Indian hospital and school just for the Jicarillas but they could also go to the public school where the towns people went if they wanted. There were only two classrooms in the building with first through fifth grade in one and sixth through eighth grade in the other. After the eighth grade, students had to commute to Santa Fe or Albuquerque which were many miles away.

I especially liked my teacher, Agapita Gomez (now Abeyta). She was Spanish, educated away from Dulce, but returned to teach at the public school. I can still remember how greatly she influenced me with her encouraging positive attitude toward all her students.

I believe in everyone's life, there enters a person who seems to be the catalyst to the path of greater learning and determination. For me, Agapita was that person.

She called me to the blackboard one morning. "Patsy, I know you can solve this math problem. Will you please come up to the board and show everyone how to do it?" I did it correctly and from that point on I had a confidence that no one could break. She was a remarkable teacher, and when I think back, I wonder how she managed to teach five different grades in the same room by herself.

Fellow followed me to school almost every day until finally Agapita suggested that we provide a desk and other things he needed and let him become part of the class until he grew tired of it. Sure enough, it did not take long before he was convinced that he would rather play outdoors than sit behind a desk all day.

As he grew older his appreciation for the classroom diminished even more and he was known, on occasion, to attend class long enough to answer the roll call and then climb out the window and spend the day in happy pursuits.

After fifty years, I found Agapita Gomez Abeyta again and had a wonderful conversation with her. She sent me several old photos of the classroom and herself. She is retired now and living just a few miles from Dulce. She has three daughters, all teachers, one named Marie who is teaching in Dulce at this time.

Chapter
7

One winter it snowed so much it seemed as though the whole world turned white. The snow reached the top of our barn and porch roof of the house. We had to have a crew come out and shovel the car out of the barn where we usually kept it.

The Apache workers piled the beautiful white stuff up very high making wonderful hills for us to slide down. We could get on the roof of the house and jump off into the snow and not get hurt.

It was grand for us but posed a problem for the train that brought all of our supplies into Dulce. It was stuck midway between Durango, Colorado, and Dulce. When a crew finally reached it, it was totally covered by snow and took days to dig it out. The snow had drifted up as high as the crossbars on the telephone poles.

The people in town were relieved to see the train pull into Dulce with fresh supplies, medicine and other necessities. It all seemed exciting to us but I'm sure the adult population could give you another reaction.

At one point, the all-important train was literally our angel of mercy. It carried Sherry to a hospital in Durango when the roads were closed due to ice and snow. She had become very ill with a high fever, earache, swollen glands and a very sore throat.

Mother was scared and Dad decided to drive them to Durango. We could only use the local Indian hospital in cases of extreme emergencies. My father did not get very far before he came upon a large hole in the road from a cave-in earlier in the day. It had filled with water which had turned to ice. They had to return to Dulce and hoped to catch the train. Sherry's condition worsened during the night so the next day they caught the train. Her temperature had risen to 104 degrees and large swollen knots had formed behind one ear.

During the three hour ride to Durango, Sherry broke out in a terrible rash and when they reached the hospital she was quarantined for three day. No one was allowed to visit her and she later told us about her sheer loneliness in such isolation. She had German Measles.

After that incident, my father had a hard time trying to convince Mother that we wanted to stay in Dulce. She was also tired of being confined during the long winter months. But on a happier note, that was the winter we discovered how to make delicious ice cream using icicles that were dangling from the roof of the house.

These icicles would sometimes reach four feet in length and we would delight in batting at them with a stick to send them hurling into the deep snow around the porch.

Sherry could not get out, so Mother used her imagination constantly trying to entertain her. It was cheap to make ice cream because milk and cream were so reasonable and easily obtained.

Our milkman could get through any weather and he would occasionally take Fellow along on his deliveries. Fellow would sit high on top of the milk jugs destined for the reservation. On occasion, Lee Martinez, another friend who worked at the store, would volunteer to take Fellow on short journeys around the Reservation.

Chapter
8

That particular winter was very hard on many people, especially Fire Man. He was always dressed the same in a red plaid shirt, dirty jeans, and a stove pipe hat. The hat had a long feather stuck in it and I thought he looked ridiculous perched high on his old black horse.

His poor old squaw would have to run through the deep snow to keep up with the horse and Fire Man would never even look back to see if she was having difficulty. You could hear him fuss at her in Apache and could only guess what he was saying. She would just run a little faster.

Very few people could handle Fire Man, but Ish Koten could. He threw Fire Man in jail regularly and his squaw would squat on the steps of the old rundown building and wait for her husband to be released. Sometimes it was days.

The Jail backed up to the edge of the arroyo and over the years the bank had been eroded underneath the left corner of the jail until it hung over the arroyo at a precarious angle. Anyone occupying the corner cell had the extra worry, besides being incarcerated, of possibly tumbling into the arroyo.

That would be an incentive for most criminals to go straight but not Fire Man. He would defiantly urinate through the cracks in the floor to the arroyo below and yell obscenities at passers by. Everyone suffered when he was in jail.

But it was all over when he came to an untimely end one day during a terrible snow storm. He could not get his usual pint of whiskey so he decided to drink rubbing alcohol. He became crazy and wild and wandered out into the snow and froze to death in the hills. It was several days before he was found but he was perfectly preserved.

There was no morgue in Dulce so he "lay in state" in the local ice house until his widow could claim his remains. She took her time but finally rode into town on his old black horse adorned in his stove pipe hat and pulling a litter behind her. I believe she was smiling.

Chapter
9

Dulce during those years was relatively crime free. There were just a few cases of trouble, usually involving whiskey. It was illegal to sell alcohol to the Indians and the closest place for them to get it was in a little town named Lumberton, New Mexico. It was usually not worth the trouble for the Apaches to go that far for bootleg whiskey but a few could not resist that "demon rum."

On occasion trouble would break out on the reservation but was quickly and quietly handled by the Indian council or the government officials in Dulce. My father was not involved very often in these affairs.

There was one occasion when Ish Koten needed someone influential with certain Jicarillas and he called upon Dad to help him with an arrest. One morning he came to Dad's office at the trading post to discuss a matter involving a young Indian from the reservation named Lucas.

Lucas would drink too much and get violent enough to start tearing up half the town. He was tall and very strong making an arrest difficult as well as dangerous.

When Lucas was sober, he was a mild mannered and treated his mother, who lived with him, with great respect. But when he was intoxicated he would be just the opposite and she would have to leave the tepee or carry a weapon to scare him off during his drunken rages.

She knew the whiskey was destroying her son. Harming Lucas with a gun or knife was out of the question for her so she usually opted to flee instead. If it was in the middle of winter, she usually came into town and stayed in an abandoned building near the trading post. If it was warm weather, she would just hide out in the mountains or at times near enough to see the tepee.

Lucas had always liked his friend, Al, so Ish Koten wanted my father to accompany him on this search and arrest. Lucas had gone too far this time and had torn down a quarter mile of fencing and had hit a cow with his truck. It was a miracle he even drove away after the collision.

Many times when someone had hit an animal that large, severe damage was done to both the driver and the animal. Running into deer was an everyday occurrence in that part of the country. Lucas had a large old pick-up truck and it had survived many "headons" with both animate and inanimate objects but he never hit another human being. His pick-up was battle scarred from front to back, like a notch on a rifle stock.

Dad agreed to leave the trading post for a short time to assist Ish Koten but he made it clear that if any shooting occurred he would head for cover. After all, he was not a trained law man and had a family to care for.

The two men had no way of knowing that during the night Lucas's mother had quietly left the tepee when she heard her drunken son returning. She took her knife, a very big knife, and she wore it stuck through her heavy concha belt at an angle so the blade was in plain view.

She came to our house. But we were all sleeping and were not aware of her presence on the side porch. She just squatted down and slept there for the remainder of the night. My father did not see her when he left for the trading post that morning or he would have taken her to the post with him for safe keeping and he would have also known that Lucas was on the war path again.

Mother got up early and started her usual day of cleaning and washing, but she did not discover the old Indian woman until she came around to the front door and looked in. She could not speak any English and it was soon evident that she was spellbound by the washing machine.

She had never seen one before and she was a little frightened at first and then fascinated by the contraption. Mother was frightened of the old woman for a moment so they just stood there starring at each other. Then Mother's eyes rested on the huge blade of the knife at the old woman's waist.

Quickly Mother took Sherry aside and told her to go to the store and get my father. Sherry ran all the way only to find that Dad had left with Ish Koten in search of Lucas.

My father and Ish Koten had gone on horseback because it would be easier to find Lucas if he was hiding anywhere near the reservation or in the underbrush along the arroyo. They had spotted the old red pick-up truck abandoned in some bushes near the arroyo and knew he could not have gotten very far on foot in his condition. He was probably sprawled in the sage brush, face down, sleeping off his whiskey.

They searched for several hours, following his foot prints which led directly back toward town. Kicking their horses into an easy gallop, they headed back down the dusty road watching for signs.

Meanwhile, Mother had managed to overcome her fear of the old woman and had tried to communicate with her. She did all the talking while the old woman just pointed to the washing machine and grunted. She clutched the knife in her concha belt which kept Mother uneasy. It was impossible to know what she had in mind.

When my father and Sherry did not come back right away, Mother got very nervous. She was reluctant to leave the old woman unattended in the front part of the house but she had no other choice. She went to the side porch and peered out to see if anyone was coming down the road from the trading post.

Suddenly Mother noticed the little barn door where Dad kept the Lincoln standing open. She did not remember my father opening it before he left. He had walked to work that morning!

Then the door moved slightly and she caught a glimpse of a man's legs and feet in fishing waders. Who was behind the door wearing Dad's fishing waders?

In great alarm, she realized in one direction there was a woman with a very big knife and in the other direction a stranger behind the barn door. She decided to gather us up and run for the post as hard as she could but just as she decided to do that, she saw my father and Ish Koten galloping toward the house.

She ran out to the gate speaking so fast it was hard for them to understand. My father had seen the old woman as they rode up so he waved to Mother to be silent and he dismounted and walked up to the old Indian. She was obviously glad to see him because her eyes brightened as he spoke to her in Apache. She answered, laughing a little and Mother realized that her fears were unfounded. After a brief conversation in Apache, she nodded her head "yes" and started off toward the reservation.

My father explained to Mother who she was and what her son had been doing and, at that moment, Mother remembered the man behind the barn door.

The feet were still there so Ish Koten called for the person to come out. There stood Lucas, looking ridiculous and guilty. He made no attempt to run, probably because he had put the waders on the wrong feet and it would have been impossible to run in that condition.

Lucas was holding an old gun, called a hog-nosed pistol, pugnaciously in his hand. Dad recognized it as one that he kept in the barn. It appeared that Lucas was not going to relinquish it without a fight but with a little persuasion from my father, he sheepishly handed it over to his trusted friend.

Dad enjoyed a good hearty laugh and then Lucas had to spend the rest of the day and night in the local jail house. I don't think he was ever cured of his alcoholism. It was a true waste of a human being because he was a fine looking man and a good son when he was sober.

Al Williams (Chief Red Eagle) Grand Marshall of Rodeo in Dulce, 1939-1941.

Ruth Williams and (left to right):
Sherry, Fellow (Chris) and Patsy.

Agapita Gomez Abeyta—teacher of five grades in one room class, 1942.

*Patsy and Sherry working hard in class.
Grades one through five represented here.*

*Al Williams
(Chief Red Eagle)*

*Al Williams favorite sport—fishing.
Borne Lake, northern New Mexico.*

Al Williams, Postmaster, Accountant and friend in his office at the General store.

General store, trading post, postoffice.
Dulce, 1939.

Ish Koten

*Chief Baltazar
with Al Williams*

Wife waiting patiently for fireman.

Main street—Dulce, 1939.

Al Williams and son storing ice for locals.

Sawing and loading ice bound for the ice house in Dulce,
Our only source of refrigeration.

Horse drawn milk wagon waiting to be loaded with milk and ice for the reservation.

Very rich Apache showing his money.

Chief Baltazar's many sheep.

*Chief Jim Baltazar
with his many
sacks of wool.*

Williams' home after a light snow.

Train pulling into Dulce on a snowy and cold day.

Snow.

Chapter
10

In some ways Dulce was civilized and in others it was primitive. We had the best of both worlds. Mother had most of the modern conveniences available at that time except for refrigeration. We had a rustic old icebox and the ice man would deliver ice to us about every other day.

Ice was actually cut during the winter from the a big lake using picks and saws. It was then transported and stored in the big ice house behind the trading post. Enough ice was usually stored in sawdust and wood shavings to last through the summer months which where relatively short in the mountains.

We had electricity, running water and modern indoor plumbing but the house next door did not have those luxuries. Our evening entertainment was a radio that provided us with "soap operas" and the usual news.

We learned to be inventive with games, story telling, candy making and such activities. We had mulberry and current berry bushes in our yard and we picked the berries for Mother to make jelly. She would also make dolls for us out of live hollyhock flowers and sew us pretty dresses.

We went on many picnics and fishing trips. Dad taught all of us to be better than average trout fishers. What a thrill it still is to this day to cast a line upstream and watch it bounce and roll across the swirling rapids and turbulent swells until it comes to rest in a quiet spot beside a big rock. Knowing almost exactly to the moment when a trout would strike, one had to be ready to set the hook.

We fished with salmon eggs for the most part but Dad used a handsome fly that he made himself. It is peaceful and theraputic to fish and one also has the extra benefit of being in tune with nature and closer to God. I do not mean, "Oh, God, please let me catch a fish," but "Thank you God for the peace and the beauty of this place."

We had other activities that involved our friends and business acquaintances such as special gatherings at the gym, town meetings, roller skating parties, and sporting events. We went to church almost every Sunday. Mother would not have it any other way. No one pushed me into believing anything. I discovered the Lord all by myself.

Once on an Easter Sunday morning, I was chosen to hold a small white rabbit in my arms during a special song. I felt its heart beating against my arm and it was so soft and warm that it occurred to me at that moment that only God could have made such a beautiful little creature.

At a later time Mother insisted that we go to vacation Bible school. Our protests were ignored. We wanted to be outside running and playing instead of being confined to a classroom drawing pictures and listening to a boring grown-up go on and on about things we did not understand.

During one of these boring moments I lapsed into a daydream and was staring out the window at the sunlight bouncing off the leaves of a huge cotton wood tree. Suddenly, I was struck by the beauty of the contrasting colors. The depth of the green trees and the brilliance of the sun and blue sky cannot be described. Somehow I was a firm believer from that day on. No mere mortal could possibly ever make anything as wonderful as that scene. It triggered a desire in me to learn more about the great and wonderful Jesus. To this day my thirst for his knowledge is unquenchable.

Chapter
11

During the warm summer nights we usually slept with our bedroom windows open and were lulled to sleep by the calls of the night birds and barking dogs in the distance. Often we heard wails of Coyotes roaming near the reservation.

On one occasion we heard the sharp cry of a mountain lion crying for her cub. It sounded like a woman screaming. Dad got up and closed the window because he felt it would be safer. The big cat might come closer than we wanted but as a rule, mountain lions did not bother people unless they were threatened.

One night I had drifted off into a peaceful slumber when suddenly the thundering hooves of many horses and the whinnying of the leader could be heard coming closer. Dad jumped out of bed and grabbed his lantern. He raced out to the front porch in nothing but his pajama bottoms.

At that moment the herd of wild horses came crashing into our yard through the swinging gate at the end of the old board sidewalk. We had left it open during the day which always concerned Mother because there were many wild dogs as well as Coyotes that would come in and she was afraid for our safety. There had been rumors of rabid animals in those parts.

There must have been fifteen or twenty wild mustangs. They ran frantically, pushing together, neighing loudly as though they were facing danger. Their erratic running, pawing the ground and stamping cut deep ruts in our newly planted yard.

The leader of the herd was a red and white patched horse and he looked no bigger than the rest but was clearly the leader as the others kept their attention on him. Wild mustangs are not especially handsome horses. They have rugged bodies and shorter legs—almost stubby compared to domestic horses. They live on range grass and endure hard winters and severe weather conditions. Occasionally ranchers in the area as well as the Jicarillas would round them up to use as working stock for rodeos and herding cattle. They were not as prone to diseases and fatigue as domestic horses.

My father shifted the lantern to his left hand to relieve the cramping in his right hand caused from holding the lantern up above his head. He was as mesmerized by the horses as they were with him. But when he shifted the lantern it spooked the mustangs more than ever and they started running wildly around the bushes and trees and banging into the fence trying to escape.

When they ran into the back yard, Dad ran for the big gate that was across the driveway. He knew they would have more room to escape through it and he kept his eyes on the leader making sure that he kept his distance. My father jumped on the big gate, released the latch and with the weight of his body caused the gate to swing wide and open all the way. He never let go of the lantern.

At first the mustangs were afraid to approach the opening because of my father and the lantern but suddenly the leader decided it was safe and he darted through with the remaining horses fast on his hooves. As they pushed through the twenty foot opening, Dad caught a glimpse of one of the prettiest horses he had ever seen. It was a roan with a long black mane flowing freely in the wind. It had gentle eyes and definitely seemed out of place with the rest of the herd.

My father said, "I would love to have you big fella," but he knew by morning they would all be back in the mountains.

I had never seen such beauty. It was such a natural and mysterious thing.

I was afraid for Dad because he obviously was more excited than the mustangs. He wasn't pleased about having to restore the yard but it was almost worth it to have been privileged to witness the "visit from the wild herd."

When morning came, Dad stood on the old worn board walk leading to the gate and surveyed the damage. To his surprise it wasn't as bad as he thought it was going to be.

He glanced across the dirt road to the left of the pasture owned by Papa John Bull and could hardly believe his eyes there was the whole herd grazing peacefully in the open field. Dad took immediate action. He started off down the road to the store walking briskly and with great determination. He was going to catch that roan.

An hour later the mustangs were still there so Dad had time to gather up some help from friends interested in rounding up a few mustangs to sell and train. Here came five horses and riders with Al Williams leading them. They were excited and ready for the chase.

They rode as quietly as possible at a slow canter but with enough momentum to break into a full run when the time came. At the end of the fence the riders separated and approached the wild herd from the north in a semi-circle.

We watched from our favorite vantage point standing on the bottom railing of the fence. Mother closed both gates and made sure they were locked this time.

Slowly the riders circled the herd and then started making noise by waving their ropes and hats and yelling. They were going to herd the wild mustangs into the south end of town to the corral that was built as a holding pen for cattle and horses waiting to be loaded onto the train. At first the mustangs ran in panicked patterns trying to escape the threatening riders but they were allowed the open end which was the intent. They ran south followed by the whooping riders straight down the middle of the road, and across the bridge where other riders were waiting to herd them into the corral.

When they were safely locked up, my father climbed up on the top rail of the corral to view his victory. His face fell. The roan was not among the others. In fact the roan was never seen again. It was a mystery. Dad got over his disappointment but never forgot the special horse that was almost his.

Chapter
12

The Jicarilla Apaches were very protective of their ceremonies. Outsiders were seldom invited to attend and then they could only view the ceremonies from a distance.

But Dad was well liked and because of his designation of Chief Red Eagle, he was occasionally invited to attend their ceremonies. He was both flattered and pleased.

One of these times was a special invitation to witness a marriage. The rest of us could not go but Dad told us as much as he could without breaking the code of privacy.

When he arrived at sundown, the festivities were well underway. The Indian maidens were dressed in their finest array and the drums were pounding out the music and rhythm to their wedding dance. Indian men were also dressed in their colorful and handsome attire, each carrying a special robe or blanket on their shoulder.

There was a large bonfire in the center of the camp that made dancing shadows on the tepees nearby. The reflected firelight gave an enchanted feeling to the surroundings.

When the dancing began, the maidens formed a circle around the bonfire with arms joined and feet moving to the steady rhythm of the drum. Their beaded jewelry and belts made eerie accompaniment to the alternate hard and soft stepping of their moccasin feet as they danced around the circle of fire.

Soon the drums stopped for a moment and the maidens sat on the ground. Then the men formed an outer circle and began their dance and chant.

Emotions showed on the faces of each of the men and women leaving Dad to assume that they had chosen their mates in advance.

When the dance was over, it seemed that they had positioned themselves directly behind their intended brides and with one gesture the men threw the robe over their sweetheart and carried them off into the night.

The ceremony was complete but the festivities extended well into the night. Dad came home feeling privileged to have been invited to this event.

Chapter
13

The road that passed in front of our house lead from the trading post where my father worked to the Jicarilla Apache Reservation. It was well traveled by the Indians and many of them were our friends and acquaintances.

Sherry, Fellow and I used to stand on that bottom railing of our fence that separated our yard from the dusty road and call greetings to them as they passed by on their horses. Sometimes they were in wagons and at times they were walking.

Our property was also one of the few sources of water for many of them and they were always welcomed to stop and fill their containers for their personal use which they did almost every day. In the winter, Dad made special adjustments to the pump to insure that it was always free running so they could have all the fresh water they needed for the harsh winter months.

Almost all of the Jicarilla lived in wigwams or tepees. They relied on small fires in the center of the wigwam for their heating and cooking needs. I used to wonder how they could stay warm when the outside temperature dropped to below freezing.

Many of the Jicarillas had adopted the ways of the "white man" due to their experience in the Indian hospital and other government supplied facilities. But there were a few who would not accept any of our ideas and clutched tightly to their traditional customs and culture.

It was one of these firmly clutched customs that almost caused the death of one of our friends and neighbors. Mrs. Jimeniz was pregnant and in labor. Several members of her family wrapped ropes around her stomach and tried to squeeze the baby out by pulling the ropes tight.

It was evident after hours of pain and agony that this was not going to work and one of her concerned relatives rushed to the trading post for help. The superintendent of the Bureau went to her home and insisted that she be taken immediately to the hospital. There was much difficulty in convincing them that this must be done in order to save Mrs. Jimeniz and her baby.

Finally, after a long time haggling over the situation, the relatives relented and put her in a wagon and took her to the hospital. It was hard for them because it went against every tradition and cultural idea that they were raised with on the reservation.

I am telling this story to impress upon my readers just how the Indians held to their way of life against all odds.

I can remember being very ill at one time with a stomach ache that seemed to last for days. Mother became worried and took me to the trading post to see my father. The Medicine Man from the reservation was sitting in Dad's office on one of his rare visits to town and he listened with great interest to Mother's detailed account of my illness.

He then came over to me and taking a black beaded necklace from around his own neck, placed it gently around mine. He said, "If you wear this every day you will be well soon."

I believed him and my stomach ache went away. His philosophy was an ancient one but it did not dawn on me until much later in life, that "belief" is a powerful medicine. I eventually gave that precious necklace to a friend but I still retain the beneficial belief in the power of the mind to heal.

Chapter
14

In the summer time we spent many wonderful days picnicking and fishing on a lake a few miles from Dulce. This lake was deep in the mountains. We seemed to wind for hours along the narrow road, past cliffs and vigilant pines that reached up to the sky. Occasionally, we would see deer standing stone still in the shelter of woods just a few yards from the dusty road. They would make no effort to run but we knew if the car stopped, they would be gone in a flash.

A small rushing stream coursed its way beside the road, changing sides now and then and sometimes we even had to drive through the stream to continue. It was only about a foot deep at that point but it was of great concern to us. We would feel the tires bumping and sliding off the slick rocks just beneath the surface of the water. The sound of the water rushing over and around the stones and rocks was audible even above the hum of the engine.

The smell of freshness was everywhere. We passed cattle grazing. They would stop eating and glance at us for a brief moment and then go back to their chewing.

Now and then Dad would stop the car and get out his fly pole. He would walk a little way, usually upstream, looking for a pooling place to cast his fly for a big trout.

My father always carried a magnificent handmade creel over his shoulder which he would layer with wet mossy grass from the stream bed. This kept the fresh trout alive until he could clean them and put them on ice or cook them.

He wore rubber fishing waders and could maneuver around and over the slippery rocks without being swept off his feet. We used to watch him in wonder as he could negotiated the fast stream without being carried downstream by the seat of his pants. But it happened once.

It was May and the water was still icy cold from the snowcapped mountain runoff and more swift than usual. He wadded out four to five feet from the bank and suddenly lost his footing and went down, fanny first. He did not appreciate our laughing and enjoying the scene while his waders filled with ice water. When this happens the rubber waders become like lead weight. He had to unstrap them and let them float away from his legs in order to stand up and get back to the bank.

But Mother built a fire and we managed to dry him out. He was a good sport about the whole thing. It was fortunate that we had blankets and food and matches for our fire. Anyone living in those mountains had to always be prepared for the unexpected so we had those things with us at all times. We learned that from the first day we arrived in Dulce.

We continued on up the mountain road until finally reaching our favorite camping and fishing spot. In a matter of minutes we were off exploring and enjoying the wilderness. It was quiet, serene and breathtakingly beautiful. There was so much wildlife in the mountains including bear, wild turkey, mountain lions or cougars, deer, raccoons and abundant fowl. We never actually saw a bear on one of these outings but we could smell that distinct odor they left behind or could tell when one was near by the same smell. We knew enough not to venture very far from the campsite.

Mother set up the table and food and started a campfire. We could smell the coffee and smoking wood. She called us to eat just as the sun was sinking behind some tall pine trees but it was still light enough to see. I selected a big flat rock to sit on with my plate balanced on my knees.

Just as I was taking my first bite of food, Dad took several giant leaps toward me and in one motion, with both hands, lifted me straight up in the air, stomping madly at the ground. I didn't have time to get scared. It was such a surprise to be held in the air by my armpits by a stomping mad man. My plate flew in one direction and my fork in the other. After what seemed like eternity, my father sat me down gently on my feet and said, "Man, will you look at the size of him!" It was a large Copperhead snake that had also chosen this rock to make his resting place. He had crawled out from under the rock just as I had made myself comfortable.

My father was always on the lookout for danger to his children and as I grew up I developed that same sense of awareness of potential danger for my children.

Chapter
15

I have written much about the winters in Dulce because many memorable events occurred during those parts of the season. Even though it was cold and long, we could devise clever ways to entertain ourselves and others. We went on sledding and tobogganing jaunts, complete with bonfires and delicious food and hot beverages. But not without some drawbacks. Our boots were fur lined and came up to our knees and still the wet snow would find its way down to the end causing our toes to ache with cold. We wore snowsuits that were fleece lined and I thought we could never get hurt with all that extra padding for protection.

Our daring at that age faded as we grew older but then we were fearless and would pile on a sled four to six people deep, and slide down a steep and slick hill. If we fell off, we just brushed off the sticky snow and got back on and continued dodging trees, bushes, and other sledders on the way down.

During one of these expeditions a woman named Marie was severely injured. She was on a four-man toboggan speeding down a steep icy slope when it overturned, hurling the riders in different directions. Marie fell face down and slid for what seemed like eternity. She was helpless to control the situation or help herself and when she finally did stop, she was covered in blood, as was the snow several feet behind her.

Her face was barely recognizable, smeared with blood and snow plastered against the wounds. She did not feel the pain immediately because the cold had a numbing effect. When she saw the trail of red in the snow, she became hysterical and went into shock. She was wrapped in blankets and rushed to the Indian hospital. The doctors said the snow acted as a good first aid and was a blessing in a way.

The treatment was much like that for a burn victim but when she healed, it appeared she would be scarred. We all learned to be more careful after that incident and the three of us were confined to the four foot hills in our own backyard for a time.

Chapter
16

Spring finally came once again and the arroyo was threatening. Dad kept a watchful eye on it all day with Corky, our dog, at his heels. The reddish brown water was tumbling and rolling debris as well as small limbs and trash which was clinging to the banks. Anything in its path would be carried swiftly far away.

Corky got too close. My father called him back with a soft whistle but suddenly Corky's hind paws slipped in some loose soil and he tumbled over and over in the mud and small rocks, falling down the steep side of the arroyo until Dad could no longer see him.

My father stood frozen for a moment in horror and disbelief and then started running toward the bridge. He remembered that there was a sandbar jutting out below the bridge where water pooled up and debris would sometimes collect there before being swept on downstream.

Maybe he could reach the sandbar and grab the dog before he was carried away. As my father reached the sandbar he saw several logs jam together and hang up on the stubby undergrowth of exposed tree roots sticking out of the sides of the bank. This snarl caught Corky.

Only his head was visible and his eyes were wild with fear as he struggled violently to free himself from the prison of tangled wood. He would sink below the surface and then re-surface with frantic clawing trying to gain control over his situation.

Dad scrambled down the embankment, slipping and sliding, and cutting his hands on the jagged rocks and sticks. The water was not rising any further on the bank and that was in his favor. Reaching the jammed up pile of debris, Dad pulled wildly at the entanglement to free the rapidly weakening dog.

The murky water made it impossible to see beneath the surface so Dad had to feel with his hands and hope for a miracle. Pulling and tugging with all his strength, he managed to separate the debris enough to grab Corky at the nape of his neck. With one strong yank and a "God please help me!" he pulled the soaked dog free and carried him up the bank to safety.

When we saw Dad carrying our dog, we ran to meet them. Mother washed and dried Corky, who was trembling violently, and talked to him in soothing tones until he calmed down. He fell asleep near the old pot-bellied stove in the kitchen, occasionally whimpering in his dreams. I am sure he was reliving his close call.

Chapter
17

Across the road from our house, there was a huge and cantankerous black and white bull. We called him Papa John Bull and I don't have a clue where that name came from. This big bull delighted in terrorizing every living thing, human or not, that passed by.

He would paw the ground, snort, and do all the things a menacing bull does. He was known as the meanest bull in the county.

One of our favorite pastimes was to throw stones and tease him unmercifully. This was a shameful thing to do, but we didn't get caught doing it so we kept it up for a while. We assumed he could never break through the barbed wire fence and go after his tormentors. But one day when one of Mother's friends was visiting, she looked out the window and saw us teasing the bull so she decided to teach us a lesson. She came across the road shaking her finger at the bull, saying something in Apache meaning, "Get out of here you mean old thing."

Now Papa John was really mad. He ran at the fence and crashed against the barbed wire so hard we thought he broke through it. He didn't but we all ran and learned a lesson that day.

Papa John got his revenge indirectly because I had many nightmares after that about his chasing me. It caused me many sleepless nights which I richly deserved.

Chapter
18

Every Fourth of July, the Jicarillas held their biggest celebration; the rodeo at which they appointed Al Williams as Grand Marshall and Judge.

I will never forget how handsome he was in his purple satin shirt with pearl buttons and his Stetson hat. He had a beautiful silver buckle that he wore with his leather belt. It was studded with large turquoise stones.

The Indians always provided him with a magnificent Palomino stallion to ride. My heart would swell with pride when I saw him leading the parade around the ring. He would lift his hat high in the air and ride that horse as a highly honored man.

This year there were many competitors. Among them was Tall Man, so named for his six foot height. His favorite event was the bull riding competition. Tall Man was physically perfect. He was extremely handsome, part Apache and part Anglo and carried his height well. It was a definite advantage.

He was also known as the reservation "Romeo." He made many hearts skip a beat and turned many a head. He wore his hair short and lived in town most of the time. He was a liaison between the government and the Indian Council as far as trading wool and other resources.

When the bull riding event was announced, we all became attentive because it was usually the most exciting and dangerous event. Tall Man was the first out of the shoot and he drew Papa John Bull! Papa John Bull was especially cantankerous this day and he twisted, jumped in the air, pawed the ground, and tried to disengage the unwelcome guest on his back.

Every muscle in his huge body quivered and jerked with his efforts. Finally, he jumped and twisted at just the right angle and off Tall Man went, sprawling in the dirt beneath Papa John's treacherous hooves. The bull was hell-bent on stomping Tall Man into the arena.

Tall Man rolled several ways trying to get to his feet to avoid being trampled. The arena workers rolled their barrels at Papa John, shouting and attempting to call his attention away from the fallen rider. But suddenly, his hooves found Tall Man's legs and we heard bone-on-bone cracking and crunching.

The bull jaunted away far enough to survey his victory. Tall Man was quickly carried out of the arena. One of his legs had been broken.

I did not understand the full impact of Tall Man's injuries. It seemed Papa John had also damaged Tall Man's private parts—rendering him totally unable to continue his reign as reservation Romeo.

Tall Man recovered but he walked with a distinct limp from that time on and never competed in rodeo events again. Nor did Papa John Bull. Papa John died a short time later from a bullet between his eyes. No one ever knew who shot him but rumor had it that a young Indian maiden was seen near the bull pen carrying a rifle. She was not smiling.

Chapter
19

Later that summer, Jim Baltazar, the Apache Chief, invited us out to his ranch to watch the sheep shearing. He was one of the richest men on the reservation because of his many sheep and his extensive land holdings.

We were allowed to crawl up on the tall board rail fence and on occasion get inside the sheep pens to play with the lambs. There were not many lambs in the late summer as spring was when most lambs were born. But hundreds of sheep were milling about and it was always fun to chase them and hear them bleat. They had a strong smell and it took Mother many washings to rid our clothes of that odor.

Jim's crew would run each sheep down a long narrow runway and then grasp them one at a time by their neck and clip the wool off in a very short time. They looked naked but it did not hurt the sheep at all.

They would stack the wool up in big gunny sacks on a large wagon bed with high sides. We were allowed to climb up and ride on the top of the pile. It was one of Dad's jobs to help count the wool sacks and enter it on the company ledger and keep track of the profits.

After work was done and the day came to a close, Jim would build a large campfire and dinner was cooked for everyone. It was delicious and the campfire coffee smelled wonderful although we were not allowed to drink it. Dad used to tell us that "It will put hair on your chest." I wonder? My father had a great sense of humor all his life. It carried him through many hard and distressing times as well as giving the rest of his family a foundation to lean on.

Chapter
20

I have spoken of the beauty of Northern New Mexico many times and I never got tired of thinking how God's creativity flourished in those mountains. You could walk through the pine woods after a fresh snow and suddenly come upon a clearing with a view so serene and majestic that even an artist would struggle to capture the essence of the beauty it presented.

A deer could stand quietly in an opening just as mesmerized with a human as you were with it. We saw entire herds many times, crossing clearings and watching carefully for danger.

Sometimes the utter stillness was overwhelming and at times only the soft whisper of the wind could be heard in the pine needles. Occasionally, limbs or pine cones would snap and fall creating a sound that could be heard a great distance

In the summer, you could look at the same clearing and see dazzling sunlight dancing off green meadows adorned with wild flowers of many colors. And always, in the distance, the royal mountains embraced the sky. There were certain high peaks that stayed snow-capped all year round.

Once on the way to a picnic, Dad drove through Wolf Creek Pass on the Colorado border and Mother was singing along with the car radio "When its springtime in the rockies, I'll be coming back to you," and Dad joined her. They had perfect harmony between them and unusually good voices. We had all started to sing when suddenly Mother stopped and remarked, "Will you look at that!" She pointed to a meadow, and we saw acres of wild irises. Deep purple and blue with lemon yellow throats. How did they get in a meadow so high up? But there they were in brilliant bloom.

Dad stopped the car so we could get a better look. Running and laughing and touching as many as we could just didn't seem enough. We were enthralled with the majesty of the moment. My father allowed us to pick a few but we were satisfied to let them stay there—free—as God intended. I secretly thought of that meadow as God's personal garden.

Chapter
21

Being wrapped in a blanket of security and oblivion in our haven in the mountains, it would have been easy to ignore world conflicts and feel isolated from responsibility. But that was not the case in Dulce.

When the war broke out in Europe and it became more and more evident that the United States was going to become involved, many of Dad's young male friends enlisted with the 101st Army Division and were on their way to Germany. Many of them also did not return.

My father came home from the store every night with a look of apprehension and worry on his face. He would turn the radio on and listen to the latest news. It changed hourly and I heard many discussions between the adults over the possibility of the United States going in for all-out war.

Dad started talking about wanting to do his part to protect his country. The prospect of his leaving us was very upsetting to Mother but she resigned herself to the possibility that it might happen. In order to keep herself busy and to aid in the war effort she organized and was chairman of the Chama Chapter of the Red Cross. They knitted sweaters, mufflers, gloves, and made and packed bandages and supplies for our men overseas.

A few months passed and life continued as usual, but Mother and Dad were talking more and more about the escalating conditions in Europe. My father was growing increasingly more serious and pensive. I could hear them talking long after I had gone to bed at night.

Sometime during the afternoon of December 7, 1941, it was announced on the radio that the Japanese had bombed Pearl Harbor and we were officially at war. Dad's face paled and he jumped to his feet. He was ready to fight.

By the next day Dulce was bristling with indignation and many men were leaving to enlist. My parents made a trip to Albuquerque where Dad attempted to enlist.

He was turned away because of asthma problems and because he had three children. The recruiter stated that if and when the situation warranted taking men with families, he could try again. He suggested that if Dad and Mother wanted to do their patriotic duty, they could always work in a defense plant.

Investigating this suggestion, they attended a training school in Albuquerque to prepare themselves for a job in San Diego, California. Dad was trained for administrative duties which put him in charge of gasoline rationing at the San Diego plant. Mother was trained for technical duties such as airplane parts distribution. We stayed with our grandmother during this time, which lasted about six weeks. She was good and thoughtful but it was not like being home in Dulce.

Fellow was very unruly during this time and he would run away frequently. He missed his Indian friends. Grandmother Beal, was a good sport up to a point, but she eventually decided she was going to have to break him from running away and hiding every day.

His favorite hideout was in her corn field. It was at least two or three acres so he could remain undetected for a long time, usually until he decided he was hungry or it was getting late. He would then saunter out as though he had done nothing wrong.

One day when he had been gone for thirty minutes, Grandmother Beal took a large wash pan and turned it over so she could beat on the bottom. She ran through the corn rows yelling and beating on that old wash pan.

Sure enough, here Fellow came, red faced and about as scared as I had ever seen him. We all had a good laugh, and I believe she cured him from running away and hiding forever.

Finally, Mother and Dad finished their training. By this time our grandmother had decided that she wanted to go to California with us. She put her house up for sale and started packing for the trip.

We went back to Dulce to pack and say our farewells to all our old and dear friends. Dad was growing anxious to get started because, by this time, he learned that many of his friends had already been killed in action. This saddened him a great deal and he grieved openly for them.

There were many questions and lots of concerns to get us packed and ready to leave in such a short time. We said good-bye to friends, pets and familiar surroundings knowing that we would probably never see most of them again.

I gave Delfina many personal items including the wonderful, magic black necklace. I have always regretted giving it away, but it brings me comfort to think it brought her good health and happiness.

Then came the day to depart. We all cried and our Indian friends were devastated to see their dear friend Chief Red Eagle, drive away. Dad did not look back. To him, this was one of those patriotic duties that his country was asking of him and he wanted to do it.

We found California very different from our quiet isolated home life in New Mexico. The people were too busy to give us the same care and direction that the Apaches had.

We were not used to all the hustle and bustle of a thriving metropolis and felt lost. But it was not long before Dad and Mother took firm hold on their jobs and we started a new life.

Al Williams was only 57 when he died in an automobile accident. He was mourned by his loved ones, but always remembered as a gentle, kind, and thoughtful man. May your spirit rest well with the Great White Father, dear Chief Red Eagle.

Perhaps this gentle and brave spirit returns to the enchanted land we all loved and remember when we were children in beautiful New Mexico.

End